NO APOLOGIES, I WANT MORE!

Reflections on Moving Towards
"This, That, or It – Our Something More"

Andrea C. Pannell

DEDICATION

I am so thankful to God for allowing me to know the most gracious, patient and merciful love I have ever known. Here is my Hallelujah Shout thanking the Lord for blessing me with His Love and allowing me to share our conversations.

I dedicate this book to my son, Shawyn, whom I love so much and who inspires, encourages and renews my hope each and every day; to my sister friends, Liza and Valerie, because without you both, this book might never have happened.

My grandparents, Earl and Winifred "Winkie" Pannell, and Charles "PopPop" and Effie "Nanny" Johnson, each have had a significant hand in teaching me to seek God first. PopPop, 95 and still living life to the fullest, you inspire and motivate me to dream bigger. I dedicate my work to you.

TABLE OF CONTENTS

FOREWORD

I have always admired my best friend Andrea and her unwavering faith, her love for her God, and the fact that she never seems to have any worries because HE had her back. Who is HE? Where is HE? Why do I not know Him, and more importantly, why am I not hearing His voice full of advice and steps to follow? Why not me God? Why won't you guide ME?!! Am I not good or holy enough? Am I too bad? Do I curse too much? Do I not donate enough?? "Answer me," I pleaded!! ….. SILENCE.

This scenario has been going on for years, waiting for a sign, an answer, a call, anything! Until I realized that what I was seeking could come in many different forms and thus feelings. Picture this: you enter a beautiful shoe store and the salesperson brings you hundreds of shoes to try on. Not only is it extremely overwhelming, but to top it all off, all the shoes appear to be EXACTLY the same, and may I add NOT YOUR SIZE. You feel suffocated by the pushy salesperson and the boxes of shoes and clutter everywhere. The fact is that while no shoe seems to fit your foot, you oblige under all the pressure and buy not one but a couple of pairs, hoping that you can WILL them to fit YOU! Well, for me, those shoes never seemed to fit.

Andrea's writings and our conversations have helped me realize that there is not a cookie cutter way to the Source (my preferred term for God). Andrea has the ability to make you feel welcomed, loved and cherished, regardless of your religious background and affiliation. She brings the true meaning of spirituality to life, in a way that is accessible to all. Her words are sewn together with love, faith and an open mind to create a beautiful blanket you can wrap yourself in while seeking and discovering your own spiritual awakening.

Liza

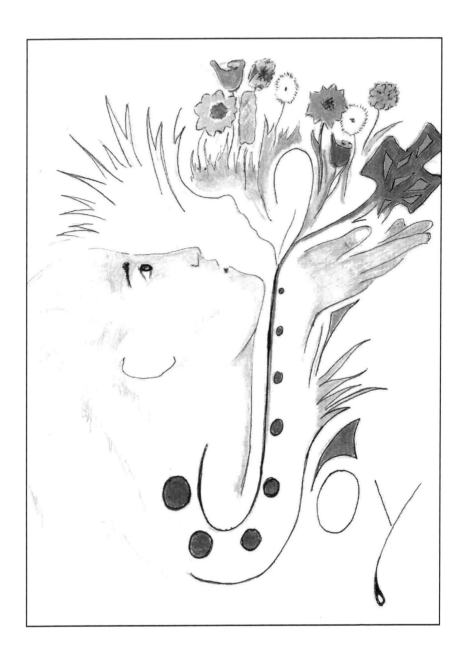

My Sacred Song of Joy

I am a woman,
a woman of vibrant color gratefully aware of
myself present to a living God!
I am a woman, a woman of vibrant color,
in celebration of my sacred connectedness
to Divine and Eternal Love.

Beautifully made,
I dare to love and be loved,
in spite of all my hurtful experiences and my perceived
failures; the betrayals I have endured and caused, and
through the wounds that life continues to pick at.

I am a woman,
a woman of vibrant color,
beautifully made and molded by the greatest
of all Loves. In spite of and because of it all,
I shall seek to embrace the beauty in me and in you, daring
to love God, myself and you fully and joyfully.

PREFACE

I finally did it! I have at last totally lost my mind and dared to share my personal thoughts and understanding of that place of mystery we sometimes call our "Something More." We have all at some point in our lives, looked at our surroundings, our job, our relationships and our lives overall, taken inventory and begun to think "There has got to be more than this, I need SOMETHING MORE."

My personal Something More journey began with a response to the unrest my friend Liza and I were experiencing, which we then named happiness without the capital H. "Capital H" Happiness then became redefined as searching for Joy and then Purpose and then the Wisdom of a Purposeful Joy. The evolution of what to call my "This, That or It" in itself was a journey and I continue to ponder and reflect on my response to "What seek ye?" (John 1:38). After years of contemplation, study, reflection and listening, for me it is seeking to simply live in the "More" space of my life where Happiness, Joy, Purpose, Love and Wisdom lovingly reside. There is no apology necessary when living from this posture of strength.

A very good friend of mine, Valerie, made a special request one day and asked me to write down some of the things I shared with her in our morning conversations. Of course I said sure, no problem, underestimating what exactly this meant for me. So, I began looking through my journals expecting to pull out a few things for her. After a few days of rereading and, quite frankly relearning, I found myself stuck on where to start and what exactly to share. The next few times I spoke to Valerie I began jotting down a note or two regarding what we talked about along with a brief reflection for me. I also began doing this with a few other friends, and before long a common theme was emerging from these notes and reflections. With a renewed clarity, I became even more aware of my own truths and the real struggle to stand in that space of abundance in which only my connection to, awareness of, and gratefulness for my need to love and to be loved authentically allows me to dwell. I was not only sharing my story I was taking a deep dive inward with every conversation.

Whether it was purpose, joy, passion, callings or whatever we were discussing, "This, That or It" always at some point demanded three things of us. Knowing who was showing up, the willingness to listen, and embracing the need to love and be loved were the gatekeepers to "More," and each step of the journey was heavily influenced and guided by personal spiritual practice. You will hear it said a thousand different ways, but knowing the truth of who shows up when your name is called, daring to love and be loved, and a willingness to listen and be present to your life each have their own breadth and depth and include multiple aspects to be considered. Collectively and collaboratively, they are key ingredients to our "Something More."

So that initial request from my very own angel, Valerie, the love of my sister for life, Liza, along with the various discussions I have had in my Circle of Sisters and with other friends and family, have been the motivation and inspiration behind writing this book. While I am excited about the opportunity to share, I am also a bit nervous about the tremendous feelings of vulnerability gripping me. Oh boy do I have a new respect for people who dare to grow authentically in front of others. I cannot claim that I have anything perfected, and I know there is much more for me to learn and discover, yet this is where I gratefully stand today. Pulling this project together has been a blessing to me. I have cried tears of hurt and joy, and laughed out loud at myself in all my silliness. I am so thankful that I took on the challenge of this experience and am grateful to my dear friend Valerie for initiating it all and my sister Liza for never letting me quit. I had no idea what I was getting myself into, and as I put the pen down for final edits, I dare to say I need just one more read-through, some further explanation and one more rewrite.

Throughout this book you are invited to take a pause and give thought and consideration to what you are reading, feeling and becoming more aware of. I encourage you to give your full attention to the emerging emotions, feelings and awareness that are surfacing. As you enter into any time of contemplation, it is always good to grant whatever freedom and permissions you will need to allow yourself to be open and attentive. I find it necessary to take from Brené Brown's instruction on granting self-permission, in her book *The Gifts of Imperfection*, and literally write out a permission slip giving me whatever I feel I need in that moment. Most often I am giving myself permission to be patient with myself. Frequently I find the need to give myself permission to take a needed "time out" and to be ok with taking a knee and a couple of deep breaths before getting back in the game.

Whether you choose to take this journey alone or with a group, I encourage you to create real opportunities for personal self-reflection time. For those reading this book as a group, this can be a challenge but is still very important. The Soul Dive Workbook was created to encourage you to travel into deeper dialog with all that may surface. While we will look more thoroughly at taking Soul Dives in Reflection 3: Deep Dive, each chapter ends with an opportunity for a compassionate discussion of self-examination and awareness. Begin by making room for it, and do not rush through this time of exploration. Initially, I found I needed at least 20 to 30 minutes of uninterrupted time with no TV or music, and phone switched off, not on vibrate but powered down, to begin a dialog with each question. This will help you to be present to the moment and the task at hand before you jump in and begin developing your response. Grab your personal journal and take the needed time to quiet your mind and spirit and ask for divine guidance as you take on what may appear right now to be a daunting task.

The reality is that we receive in as many ways as there are people in the room. So determining how best to use the information and resources within these pages will ultimately be for you to decide. I strongly encourage you to allow yourself the opportunity to revisit the wisdom in the writing, scribbling and doodling you will enter into your journals as often as you feel necessary. Your responses and awakenings that will happen throughout this time may be surprising, enlightening and even scary. Just know that as uncomfortable as it may be at times, the story being revealed to you is only to help you grow in acknowledging not only who you are hoping to become, but also the wonderful you standing here today.

I pray that this is a great read for you and that you receive the blessing and gift of encouragement to trust yourself enough to move towards your own "This, That or It." I pray that you receive all the wisdom that your own personal journey will offer to you in love. Yes, there is more and your "More" is here and patiently awaiting your full attention.

NUGGETS

I was sitting in a Public Relations Seminar about seven or eight years ago and the presenter stressed to us the importance of "knowing our nuggets." Our presenter that day was a public relations professional who had worked in many stressful and controversial situations. He shared with us that "nuggets" are the golden tickets that will ensure the message we intend to share is heard above all the rhetoric and alternate agendas. Your nuggets keep you from being steered or taken down a path where you would rather not go. He said our nuggets should be short concise clearly worded statements that are easily repeated and hopefully memorable. Our tool belt for life should be filled with hardware created from significant statements of truth; our own Nuggets for life. Just like public relations nuggets, our own personal life Nuggets should be developed collaboratively and be mission and vision driven. What makes a significant difference between PR nuggets and our Life Nuggets is with whom we are collaborating and developing our Tools and Nuggets with.

My life-giving Nuggets are a gift and not mere statements or ideas that I came up with on my own. It was during a time of study, unceasing prayer and openness that I know God gifted me with each of my gems of Wisdom, Hope, Faith, Mercy and so much more. These life sustaining Nuggets are gems I hold precious and keep securely tucked in my tool belt. My Nuggets continue to reveal themselves to me, and I continue to work at remaining open to prayerfully grow in the wisdom of each of them. Each Nugget is a dynamic living and breathing priceless gem of my faith traditions and teachings. Your Nuggets cannot be based in one-shot beliefs or ideas that have no life or truth beyond the paper they are written on. While I do not believe there is a single way to develop your tool belt, I do believe, each Life Nugget must come from a practice of authentic love. A love rooted in faith, hope, mercy, and forgiveness which for me, is Love defined in and by my intimate and personal relationship with God.

I started this part of my journey with my own need to respond to two basic questions – "Who is God for me?" and "What keeps me from or hinders me being present to this Higher Power of Divine Wisdom, Mercy and Love; to God present in my life?" Responding to these questions has become an unceasing prayer for guidance into understanding, and has definitely been the source and creator of my entire tool belt and the life giving hardware and priceless gems it holds.

Try answering these two questions for yourself in response to what you know and are witness to, not just what you have been told or have heard. It is a powerful exercise. Your "This, That or It" will demand that you explore how and where that which is greater than yourself

– the Divine Wisdom and Divine Power in your life – reveals itself, speaks to you, shows up, and exists in your life. Joy, purpose and wisdom always summon us to be attentive to the life we are standing in right now, calling us to take a look at life and relationships as they are, not as what we hope they will be within a five-year plan. Become connected to, aware of and grateful for your right now. It is here that you will find all that you need to live from a place of so much more.

Now take a deep cleansing breath and let us take our first dive into self-reflection.

How is God present in your life? What keeps you from or hinders you from becoming more present to God?

REFLECTION 1: SOMETHING MORE

*There is an unceasing longing to connect to, grow in awareness of,
and be grateful for the inherent divine reality that our
cultivated reality tends to contradict.*

Destiny, purpose, spirituality, joy, and love are all terms that our society throws around too loosely. We have diminished their importance and turned them into buzz words included in the titles of our 21 days to gain this and the top 10 list of that. Whether we call it discovering our destiny, finding joy or falling into purpose we have a divine reality of "This, That or It" we continue to long for. This unceasing yearning can be and often is in conflict with what our culture has deemed important and worthy of our time and effort. Society and the culture many of us now live in, would much rather you focus on what to "do" next and give little or no attention to who you hope to "be" moving forward. And while many of us may not know what our "This, That or It" is, we do recognize that we have a deep yearning for Something More, but for more of what? For my bestie Liza and me, we initially named our Something More Happiness.

Probably the biggest challenge in sharing this reflection with you has been in how I recognize and honor the source of my joy, purpose and wisdom. As I began to share some of my thoughts and writings with my closest friends, one of them asked me a question that has helped me more than even she is aware of. Her words to me were, "Do you think using the word "god" will turn some people off?" I now look back at the months that followed this significant question, and I hear the loud yet gentle whisper of my Creator saying "Do you love me?" and me saying in response, "Of course I do, I love you more than anything." I then have a flash of the Apostle Peter, out of fear, denying the one he followed and the cock crowing, and so I choose to respond again, "Of course I love you, and I also trust you!"

Trying to make sense of my life and where I find myself today, without mentioning the God in me and for me just became ridiculous. Finding the words to express and share this continuing journey in a way that neglects to fully recognize the One who offers this precious gift to me, would be sharing only part of the story. Ignoring the spiritual nature within any part of this journey is just not possible. You can critique, judge and argue points within this reflection if you like. As a matter of fact, please do. But there is one point that cannot be challenged: this is my reality and my truth as it is gifted to me. I help no one and this reflection means nothing if I am not honest and willing to honor my own truth and the God in it. My willingness to acknowledge and experience God was and still is a non-negotiable in living out my "Something More." I realized early on, this is not a journey I am expected to travel on my own or a destination I am meant to enjoy alone. Practicing the humility and compassion reflected in a spiritual practice that you are willing to live out and be accountable to is critical to a successful journey into "Something More."

It was a normal Sunday night conversation for Liza and me. Still today, we spend Sunday nights reconnecting, updating each other about our children and venting our thoughts and opinions on the happenings of our week and in the news. But this time we ended our fellowship not with a casual "talk to you tomorrow," but instead we were entering into a pact with one another to find our "capital H" Happiness. I am still not clear on where or when the conversation took this turn that evening, but it did, and we were now agreeing to make a special effort to find our Happiness. We both agreed that things were not bad at all for either of us, and we acknowledged our gratitude for the love of our family and friends and the many ways we had been and were still being blessed in our lives. So for all intents and purposes we felt we should be among the happiest, but we were not. This was a desire we both recognized was not rooted in our lack as much as it was a calling to "Something More." I must pause here and say that while we did feel a need for more, we laughed at ourselves because we also knew that as we had grown older, the highs needed not be so high and the lows were prayerfully not so low that we could not find a way to get back up. So while we did feel the yearning for Something More, we had to admit that we were very thankful for the uneventful days, which for me often ended with a glass of Moscato Asti in my favorite wine glass and a bit of mindless

TV watching. Still Liza and I were determined to develop a plan to get our Happy life, and yes I said plan. Of course I was expecting some ready-made step-by-step plan to surface, from wherever, for me to work at and poof, Happy life here I come. I mean I did plan on doing the work; I just needed to know what to do and the steps to take.

This life changing conversation happened the first week of my new life in Charlotte, North Carolina. I had moved down South to marry a man I met online. He really was a good man and not an online crazy person at all. As a matter of fact, I believe he is now happily married to someone else. He was a fireman and worked at night. So there I was, alone in a different state, away from all my friends and family, with no distractions and ready to go after my Happiness. I found myself in what I had determined were the perfect conditions and was ready to start developing my step-by-step plan. Liza and I both decided that we first needed to define "capital H" Happiness for ourselves beyond Webster's Dictionary, and so the very first step I took was to look to my Bible. I was sure that somewhere within the teaching offered in Sacred Scripture, I would not only define "capital H" Happiness, I would also find a step-by-step plan. So every night when my then-fiancé left for work, I would set up my study space at the dining room table and get to work. It was right there at that large wooden feast table that I found my definition for Happiness and my five-step plan for getting there. Well not really. Now hold on saints, before you stop reading and toss this book in the trash, hear what I am saying. I pray that if those reading this book do not get anything else from this reflection, they take with them this: when you have resolved in your mind what you are worthy of receiving, everything in this universe will collaborate to offer you just that, whether it be good or bad. What you see yourself deserving of, most assuredly shall be yours and what you believe yourself to be, will be validated. I am saying that in all the Wisdom and Truth that the Holy Scriptures offered me, at this moment in my life, what I received was only my five-step plan to achieve a Happiness I could understand.

I am so grateful that even the smallest of cracked doors is all the invitation God needs to continue a good work in our lives. We can be our own greatest barrier. I can now see that because steps were all I was asking for and ready to receive, I alone had limited and narrowed the gift I was being offered. What I first considered my five-step plan to Happiness, has become significant and powerful statements of truth to live by. What the Holy Scriptures had given me were greater than mere steps to follow. I was being introduced to my Nuggets of Divine Truth.

My Nuggets are the foundation of every life-giving tool in my tool belt, that I greatly depend on and trust in today and that define the "Something More" I yearn for. Highlight this one friend, KNOW YOUR NUGGETS. They will give you the tools needed to help you clear the brush, paint the sunlight on cloudy days, repair the broken stones, and lay new foundation when needed along the pathways before you in this journey. You know you have found a true Nugget, when in all that you are reading and hearing on the subject of "This,

That or It," it maintains its value, validity and integrity without distortion.

As I have been met with difficult roadblocks and warning signals, my Nuggets have given me whatever tools I needed to endure the necessary course corrections we all must face. These powerful Truths always guide me back to the purpose-driven highways and byways of my "This, That or It." My Nuggets are precious gifts of roots that have taken hold and continually nourish and provide me with a solid foundation of enduring strength. My personal Life Nuggets are:

1) God must be experienced
2) What you seek cannot be ambiguous
3) The masks must fall
4) The entitlement attitude must be abandoned
5) Prayer is a way of being

Growing in understanding of your Nuggets alone can be life-changing and tender you an enduring joy that will permeate your entire life, thoughtfully peeling back the layers of your "Something More." True Nuggets call you towards greater self-awareness and accountability and demands a willingness to be honest with yourself in acknowledging who is showing up when your name is called.

Yes, my Nuggets were setting me free. Free to stand in a Happiness I did not have the day before. I had been given the clarity to see a reality I now had to come to grips with, as I approached week four of my move to Charlotte. This fireman was going to be a great husband, but he was not going to be my husband. Just as clearly as my Life Nuggets were being revealed to me, so was my need to return home to Columbus, Ohio.

My Nuggets had begun to redefine my desire for a Happy life and gifted me with a newly discovered Joy. I was learning that while happiness comes and goes, Joy is a way of being that bestows a peace and strength beyond our understanding. I define Joy as the spiritually inspired power to live in the freedom of a divine interdependency between our individual imperfection and God's perfect love for each of us. With all that I was feeling and growing in awareness of, I was also learning how to be within this new strength taking hold of my life. I quickly realized that this was just the beginning and that there was much more ahead. I was not there yet and little did I know God was not done with me yet.

I was given a prayer a few years ago that ended with "The will of God will never take you where the GRACE of God will not protect you." I do not know who authored this beautiful wisdom, but there is a comfort within these words that I hold on to even today. Beginning with those thirty days of study in North Carolina, the feelings that began to arise inside of me caught me off guard then and comfort me today. Joy will initiate a stirring from the very core of your being and a knowing that you are being called to a deeper understanding and relationship with Something More. My Nuggets cleared my vision, enabling me to see that I not only wanted, but needed something greater than happy moments for myself; I needed Something More.

I needed to rediscover the heartfelt belly laugh I owned as an infant and the sense of awe and wonder I had as a two-year-old seeing my first Christmas tree. I needed to experience again and again the unexplainable peace that I felt one chilly Saturday morning while sitting on my back porch in my pajamas with only a hot cup of coffee to warm my hands and soul. I was being stirred and lifted in a way I had not known before. I could not explain the feelings then, but now, I know the awe and wonder of journeying towards my most authentic self and bestirring a joy summoning me to something much greater than I had imagined. That which is greater than I alone, the loving God I was discovering, was with me, in me and surrounding me, and offering more than I could ever imagine. My purpose, my joy and my wisdom were surfacing from within me and I was being called to rise and greet them with a simple hello.

The word bestir is a word that we rarely use anymore. It is an Old English word created to help us acknowledge when a person is stirred up or aroused from within. Bestir speaks to being self-inspired, rather than motivated by some outside influence. It is a word that I feel speaks genius-ly (yes, an Andreaism) when we are trying to describe the stirring from within calling us to Something More. We bestir ourselves to move with the call into a renewal of sorts, a revealing of who we are when stripped down and standing bare.

I know for some this sounds scary, and it is. Daring to face your Something More can be intimidating and you will no doubt endure a number of cuts and bruises along the way. This is where we must learn not to run away but to faithfully lean in with our Nuggets in hand – lean into the discomfort and even the pain and hurt of disappointment and betrayal. It is in these uncomfortable and painful moments that we find our greatest opportunities for growth. An elder once told me, "Andrea, iron sharpens iron." She continued, "How do you come to appreciate the light if you have no experience with darkness? How do you come to cherish true friendship if you have never been hurt by a friend's deception and betrayal?" Painful moments are necessary and hurt is unavoidable yet fear, guilt and shame should not be your motivation or dwelling place.

So here I am with my Nuggets securely tucked in my tool belt and an enthusiastic "yes" to the vision of my "Something More," but now how do I get there? I had read lots of books and took every magazine quiz I could find on happiness and finding passion and discovering purpose. All of them offered me some tidbits of information about myself. I found Jennifer's 10 steps to happiness that worked for her and Daniel's 21 days to finding his purpose planned out for him. But again, with my Nuggets in tow, I was back to asking "Where is Andrea's step-by-step plan?" "Where was the plan I could follow and master?" Well, I can tell you I did not find my step-by-step, and I surely have not mastered anyone's plan to finding "This, That or It." What I did discover is that what I was searching for, no one could give me, and there would not be a simple step-by-step process for me to follow.

It had come time for me to put down the self-help books and the expectation of a pre-planned process and take the necessary deep dive inward. Nearly everything I had read, and all my spiritual teachers, leaders and counselors had shared with me, told me that at some point the road to "This, That or It" comes with a mandatory compassionate and loving dive into self-scrutiny. It will not be pretty or painless they all promised, but it is unavoidable. My Grandma "Winkie" would say, "The only real pain in this life is growth," and now I myself can testify to this. For the sake of our own truth and growing in our cognizance of our Something More, we must allow the tears to fall knowing our perceptions, understandings, relationships and even a few things we hold sacred must die or be left behind. Have you ever noticed how quickly your memory of a dream fades away after you wake up? This will also happen as you begin to rise to meet your own highest potential. With every awakening there comes a fading away that you must allow to happen.

I don't know how anyone can take on this challenge without the faith and knowledge of a much greater love and mercy offered to them. The unknown can be a scary place, but revisiting disappointment can be terrifying. As adults, revisiting the dreams and aspirations we had as children can be a history we are not ready to face. As simple as this may seem to some, the disappointment of dreams deferred and desires dismissed can keep us from delving beyond the surface of our view inward. We then build a room wallpapered with our defeats, weaknesses and humiliations that we have learned to hold sacred. We refuse to ask for or consider owning anything we cannot acquire on our own with the least amount of pain and can find ourselves dwelling in the false security of self-reliance. Some of us have forgotten how to dream altogether and find ourselves irritated by and judgmental towards those who dare to look beyond the shore.

So as I took my deep dive, my dreams became clearer, the desires of my heart were validated and my Something More began the big reveal. I yearned for the enlightened heart vision that Paul spoke of in his letter to the Ephesians, and the peaceful awareness of sacred connectedness with all things I felt reading Native American traditions and wisdoms. I yearned to be contemplative and mindful of each moment like the Zen Buddhist Monks and to twirl with abandonment of all insecurities as if I were a Sufi whirling in meditation and devotion to God. Yes, this was the More calling out to me and I wanted all of this. But was this all possible for me? What do I call this all, this More that my Nuggets continue to reveal to me? Is this my purpose, my destiny, finding wisdom or joy, and what do I do now? With this I lifted my head and looking towards the clouds I gave out a big hallelujah to the heavens above. I was no longer naive to the understanding that this was no easy 1-2-3 plan ahead. I felt in my bones that I was no longer at the beginning of my journey, while at the same time I was in full awareness that I was also nowhere near the end.

Take three deep cleansing breaths and let us take our next dive into self-reflection.

Can you imagine God saying to you "{ your name here }, lets You and I create something together?" Can you name the desires and passions at the very center of your heart?

(For an even deeper dive into self-reflection refer to the workbook at the back of this book starting on page 54 after each reflection chapter.)

REFLECTION 2: DARE TO LOVE

My purpose, my wisdom and my joy
will be revealed to me the moment I bravely look
towards love and dare to say "Hello."

Love, purpose and joy are words that are often carelessly misused and recklessly abused, causing many of us to become numb to all their truth. How we love has become distorted to fit within the false allegations of our own emotional paucity, and from this place of deficiency we struggle to dare to love and be loved. These walls –Love Limits – erected from hurtful, deceitful and abusive relationships in the name of love, limit our capacity to enjoy the fullness of love and ultimately life. Your purpose, joy, destiny or however you define "This, That or It" all have a vast dimension that is realized primarily within your aptitude for authentic love. There is mutual dependence within love that you can remain ignorant to when you view love in terms of solely what you need, or even worse, what you feel you deserve.

When we fail to be accountable to our love limits, meaning having a sincere knowledge of what we are capable of as well as incapable of offering, we can fall into an entitlement trap. Entitlement says I see value in it and have judged myself deserving of it, and therefore, I should have it or benefit from it regardless of current ownership or my ability to bear the weight of it. When we dare to love authentically we see the value in it and ourselves worthy of it, gratefully knowing that we are never burdened with ALL we deserve. I dare to love when I see all that is available to me and feeding my soul, desires and passions, even as your cup runs over, understanding that I will never need to steal from your cup to fill my own. There is no scarcity when we trust in love to live fully.

This attitude of entitlement will guarantee moments of disappointment in ourselves and others, because it fails to see the dependent relationship of loving and being loved. Our ability to give and receive expressions, feelings and acts of love are equally important to both sacred connectedness and our ability to make the necessary deep dive into our "This, That or It." We cannot offer what we do not possess even when we are "masked." Masks are the false securities we clothe ourselves in to protect our vulnerable places. At times the masks we find ourselves hiding behind must fall away and we must stand in the vulnerability of love. Love is a divine thread that weaves its way through nearly every expression of faith and spirituality in our world today. Most established religions, faith practices and belief systems will point to a critical need for love when making the attempt to reach any level of peace, joy and enlightenment. Love stretches us and affords us the needed space to explore life in a passionate and all-embracing way. Can you remember a moment when you felt the intensity of being loved and having someone to love? Remember the moment as parents when you looked into the eyes of the purest of unconditional love in your infant daughter or son? Do you remember that in each of these moments, every lack you stood with seconds before seemed to dissipate, and the magnitude of every issue and problem suddenly decreased in comparison?

The purest of love strips us down and clothes us in an unwavering and boundless joy, yet we create counterfeit limits and flounder under the burden of previous failures and disappointments in the name of love. It is only when we venture closer to the edges of our love limits that we are privileged to experience a whiff of the longings haunting us. Love inspires, empowers, heals and provides the good soil for creativity to happen. Our perceived lack is reduced to a grain of sand from a viewpoint of love, and we feel the abundance of all that love offers us. It is in this place of abundance, of our Something More, that we find "This, That or It" waiting for us.

The fear of not being loved is where we feel our most intense level of deficiency, often fueling the motivations behind our self-destruction, pain and sickness. I personally believe that love does not make a person hurt another; it is the fear of being unloved that drives a person to act out with hurtful insecurity. Knowing this, we spend very little time understanding our perceptions, responses and vulnerabilities to the innate desire to love and be loved. We choose to live by trial and error alone, often staying in an unhealthy relationship too long or being disappointed with someone's inability to change to meet our needs in the name of love. Then out of this place of deficiency and suffering, we erect a wall built with the false idea that love only hurts, kills, and steals from us. So, does love require us to continually allow someone to hurt us and take from us, in the name of patience, compassion or giving of ourselves? No, it means the very opposite. Love requires us to fearlessly stand in the truth that love is not destructive, violent or riddled with insecurity; in knowing this we can say "I will not ignore or tolerate your abusive or destructive behavior or disrespect. In other words, I love us both enough to let you go and walk away."

It is amazing that we can clearly see this with our children when we, out of a deep love for them, refuse to sit by and watch them disrespect themselves or us as parents, but will, in the name of love, allow a partner to live outside our boundaries, as hurtful and destructive as it may be. The strength of our love stance and how we choose to show up is greatly influenced by self-awareness and self-acceptance rooted in truth. With tools in hand, we must be willing to show up to love, risking rejection, hurt and disappointment. Failing to do so opens the door for fear, guilt and shame to show up and show out in love's absence. The real source of our heartache and defeat comes in the time of cleanup and dealing with the aftermath of their shenanigans, and so we vow to never love again.

With a grateful knowing that all things have purpose and meaning, a revelation of authentic love must take hold of us. The deep yearning for Something More is made known in every experience that challenges us to venture beyond our self-imposed limitations with a daring notion to stand in love yet again. There is an embrace of the very uncertainty of love itself that must happen when stepping into our Something More. It is also an awakening to knowing that what we do with our lives each and every day matters. I was reading a daily meditation one morning and this thought pierced my heart: *"What if my sole purpose for being born into this world is to be present to the Creator's landscape of sacred connectedness which enables me to answer the call to love when the opportunity arises?"* Can I let you in on a pretty big secret that many know about yet often dismiss? There is always more going on than what you or I witness, and while it is all about a love eternally present to you, it is not always ALL about you. With a blessed assurance we grow in our connectedness to one another and to that which is greater than any one of us alone. You are not in this alone and I am not in this alone, and it is here in our connectedness that a great love is offered to each of us. Our willingness to be present to our oneness, one to another and to a love greater than any one of us individually seals our agreement to an extraordinary reality of Something More.

An exploration and reconciliation of how we love ourselves, our family, friends and neighbors and God must happen. We must answer the question, "How do I answer the call to love and be loved?" Paul defines what love is and what love is not for the people of Corinth, and proclaims that without the intention of love, our acts and daily doings mean nothing. He tells them and teaches us that love bears all things, believes all things, hopes all things, endures all things and never fails (1Cor 13). Authentic love is all of these things for each of us and not a distorted excuse to endure deception, abuse, mistreatment and hatred.

It is in this love that we have the strength and courage to say, with no apologies, I am worthy of More. This will not always feel spiritual, but to find our self beyond the fear of all deficiency is our greatest spiritual practice and our fiercest posture of an all embracing love. Again, a sense of entitlement only reinforces our limitations and stifles our ability to receive and offer boundless love. I will repeat this 10,000 times until we get it. TRUE LOVE IS NOT enduring hurt for the sake of feeding into insecurity, or claiming false hope in a hopeless situation out of a fear of being alone. This full embrace speaks to bearing the weight of courage and bravery, believing and trusting in the wisdom of Divine Truth resting in you, and enduring the sometimes painful losses that come with this growth. The spirituality of love is a living and active response we are to answer within every aspect of our lives, relationships, experiences and faith movement.

I was speaking to a woman who said, "My purpose is to be a mother." She shared with me how she has become the surrogate, adopted or replacement mom to so many young people. She herself has three grown children but feels her work with the youth ministry at church fulfills her life purpose of mothering. Mothering is where Sheila loves and feels loved best. It is where she best lives out her Something More rooted in love. Philip is a man who says he has found his greatest joy in music. Music breathes life into his very soul, and without music he feels he would die. He is a fantastic musician who says he would play for free if no wanted to pay him because it is not about the money for him. Truly music is Phil's passion, he loves it, he gets paid to do it and many people feel touched by it. But if Phil lost his ability to play music and Sheila did not have anyone to mother, does this mean their entire purpose for living would cease to exist? No, because your life as well as your deepest yearnings are not anchored to any single activity, skill, talent or person. They are always connected to and defined in relationship to and with, a great and purposeful love.

Music is where Philip loves and is loved best. Mothering is where Sheila loves and is loved best. It is where they feel the joy of a love greater than any of us can fully explain or experience anywhere other than in our relationship with authentic love itself – with God. Discover the hallowed love song of your heart, your authentic voice and give yourself permission to take an even deeper dive into love, tasting the fruits of your More.

Take a deep breath of daring love and let's dive.

How am I called back to the Love I came into this world knowing; authentic love? How can I begin to trust in this love more?

(Refer to the workbook, pages 57-58, for an even deeper dive into self-reflection.)

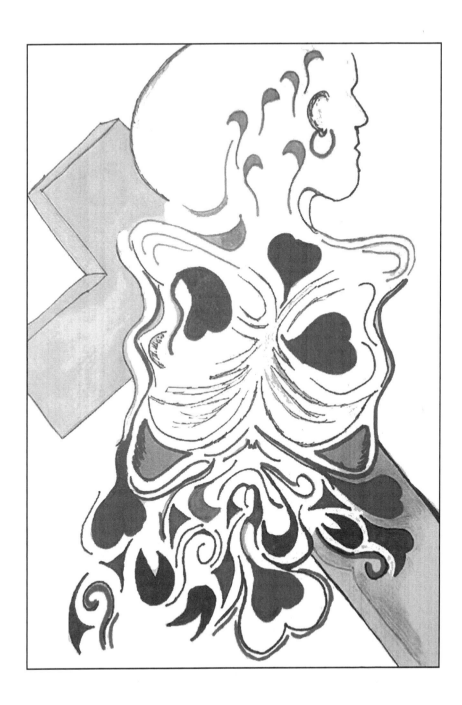

REFLECTION 3: DEEP DIVE

The road traveled in joyful purpose
will most certainly gift you with a selfie.
Who I am and where I stand today is an unavoidable
reality I shall find the courage to embrace.

We are all birthed into this world with a yearning which we are encouraged to ignore for one reason or another. A yearning that some refer to as a holy longing or a deep desire for authentic love and belonging. It is a yearning we then later in life, find ourselves blessed with the challenge of rediscovering, recognizing this neglected space in our lives to be essential to living from our fullest potential. This "dig" of sorts, expresses a need for excavation and mining for the treasures we have buried within us. In essence this deep dive is what I call taking a Soul Dive. While it would take more than a few paragraphs to even begin a conversation articulating the nature, relevance and meaning of the soul, sincere self-reflection allows us a deeper dive towards our most authentic way of being. This very courageous dive into the soul enlightens the heart and ultimately awakens us to our best self and the possibilities before us. Interestingly enough, our best self is not always who is showing up when our name is called. We find ourselves responding from a position of fear, unforgiveness and insecurity which keeps hidden away the very heart we are trying to awaken to.

This pilgrimage of rediscovery is often a very personal and intimate walk into unanticipated emotions, memories and awareness. In some cases, we are not totally prepared for all that a soul dive exposes to us, and avoidance may seem like a legitimate option. Well, it is not. Can you hear my buzzer going off and a big "wrong answer!" in my best TV game show host voice? Delving beneath the surface of our desires, passions, fears, and losses should be a dive that encourages unconditional love, primarily of self. It is not an exercise in beating yourself down, throwing salt into old wounds or exposing your flaws to make you feel defeated. Instead, a deep look inward calls us to tend to our wounds, address our inner conflicts and do what is needed to forgive, not with the intent to destroy but rather to heal and build us up, giving us the strength and courage to love and trust again. Given our limited vision and awareness, we can be quick to sentence and punish as we see fit. This judgement is not reserved only for others we see as deserving. More often than not, swift and harsh judgement becomes self-imposed punishment based on what we have come to accept as right and just. For many of us, forgiving and trusting ourselves is our greatest challenge and our greatest barrier to realizing the full power and wisdom of our own Nuggets.

If you are not familiar with the poem "The Cookie Thief" by Valerie Cox, please Google it. This is a very telling poem about how we hold on to our truth with a tight fist, refusing to entertain any alternative notion, and then making judgments on ourselves and others from this rigid stance. The somewhat harsh reality that we all eventually come to terms with is, "Your truth is 'the truth' until it isn't any more." Do you remember when you believed in the Tooth Fairy? Santa Claus? That you were fat wearing a size 6? Ha! I wish I could get into a size 9 right now, but that is another book for real!

As we begin a dive into deeper self-reflection, our love limits gradually fade and we become positioned for an intimate face to face with our "This, That or It." Yet we can still miss what is right in front of us. Have you ever looked for a set of keys that you were actually holding in your hand, or found yourself at a gathering of friends looking around the room for the person standing right next to you? You can become blind to your own truth staring you down in this same way. Widening your scope of understanding and acknowledging your current position can and will shake you a bit, and this is not a bad thing. Coming face to face with your most authentic self, your best self, can appear to be a new relationship between complete strangers, a relationship you must bravely regain trust in.

Your dive experiences will assuredly take you to places you would rather skip or detour around. But detours must be considered with caution, understanding that in most cases, you will find it necessary to circle back and revisit that same cross in the road. We must know that coming into relationship with our Something More, gifts us with an accountability that bears a weight we may not initially be so grateful for. But it is here that the brilliance of our gems for life shine their brightest and we gain the strength to stand in our "This, That or It." You see even when growing in our knowledge of what we are searching for, things do not always reveal themselves as we anticipate. But the scrutiny itself will empower and encourage you to continue, and with greater understanding, it becomes harder and harder to settle for the "sounds likes," "looks likes," and "tastes likes" that will continue to show up.

Our best plans often fail because of our unwilling-ness to acknowledge where we are starting from. I had to ask myself the question and be willing to stand in the humble honesty of "Whom do I stand as today?" Looking openly with loving compassion at just who is looking back at you in the mirror, not just once but at various times throughout this journey, will be critical. As adult men and women, most of us are very familiar with the annual exam or the yearly health screening by our medical doctor. This annual checkup helps to determine the state of our current physical health. We would not look to test results and data from a physical exam taken ten years ago or ten years into the future to determine our prescription needs of today. So we understand that a critical look at our current interests, relationships, beliefs and dreams, best aid us in planning a purposeful journey for the self we are today. Passage into our More is significantly impacted by who we are today, even more than who we look to become tomorrow.

As I mentioned earlier, there was a revelation that I had to step into, that challenged my way of being to the core. In my initial search for "capital H" Happiness, becoming aware that my own fears, guilt, shame and insecurities are what ultimately limited my ability to receive what God was offering to me was hard to swallow. My self-constructed walls and distrust had affected my ability to love and be loved and kept me hidden from my "This, That or It." This was very hard to hear and acknowledge. Not honoring and trusting in the wisdom and love God had given me, had become my greatest stumbling block.

Walking into this journey, I did not have the confidence of my own wisdom, and so I looked to trust in those I saw as wiser than myself to not only tell me what to do, but also how to be. And while we are always learning and discovering, we all come to a point where we must begin to find the courage to trust in the Nuggets we have been given. I had to find the courage to admit that I was looking for a step-by-step plan that could be manipulated to serve to my lack and became focused on gaining outlined steps to follow. But it was a very wise woman who helped me see that in focusing on the paths of others, I was falling short of the desired path being revealed to and for me. I felt a subtle yet unassailable uneasiness as I became more and more aware of my current posture. The looming doubts of "Can I?" and "Am I?" were creeping up within me. Each Soul Dive provided a courageous conversation that reinforced the truth that this was my pathway to be found, imprinted with my DNA only.

Could I do, was I willing to do, and what would I be asked to do, to deserve all that my Something More appeared to be offering to me? It was not until I stopped looking to confirm my own ideas and thoughts of what I could and could not bear that a greater wisdom within me began to gift me with a new set of eyes. Only then could I trust in myself and see my life beyond all that I felt I was not. It will always be with restored vision and wisdom that you will begin to see past your lack and what you have judged yourself as deserving or not deserving of. Only then will you attain the clarity needed to see all that is present and available to you. The moment you stop trying to focus the lens DOWN to your standards and allow the full picture to reveal itself to you, will you then fully enjoy the sacred love and hope found in "This, That or It," calling you to Something More.

Taking a Soul Dive is not something someone else can do for you or tell you step-by-step how to get through. These are your hills to climb, valleys to cross and deserts to survive. You will set the pace, choose the roads to travel and determine who will reach the final destination. Do not be discouraged when the results of your Love Limits begin to show up. Here is where my Life Nuggets offer me the lifesaving vest I often needed to keep me from drowning. You see, when self-doubt, fear and guilt begin to rear their devilish heads, we tend to quickly put on the appropriate mask of false security. Our Love Limits will stop us in our tracks as we attempt to take a step beyond the boundaries our past hurts and disappointments have helped to create. This is when I hold tightly to my Nuggets and, often with wobbly knees and a scream for help from within, I allow the masks to fall, abandon the attitude of entitlement, and ask for what I want. Many times throughout my dives, and still on any given day of the week, I must remind myself that my life is a collaborative masterpiece of my yes and my no to God's

Love and Wisdom in me and for me. It is only here, in this Truth, that I am made whole and perfect. So, I am where I am supposed to be, given the decisions I have made and allowed to be made in my life. I must remind myself that many of my bad decisions were made from within the boundaries of my Love Limits and not in the freedom of my own loving wisdom. I maintain that all my bad decisions and perceived mistakes are opportunities for growth and not defeats to be masked.

The reality is that yes, there are some things that will cross my path that I cannot control, but I always, always, always have a choice as to how I respond and how I live through it. Being able to fully and wholeheartedly receive this lesson is what supports me through every soul dive I make, and moves me from surviving to thriving in response. No, we cannot rewrite the truth of our history but we can live out a brilliant ending of our choosing. There is always a greater story rooted in love being revealed, whether you choose to be aware of it or a witness to it!

Your authentic desires and yearnings are part of the inherent dignity that you come into this world with and that cannot be denied by anyone except you, yourself. As you allow your heart to stir and your soul to be lifted by authentic love, your posture becomes one of empowerment. Obstacles are surmountable and new pathways appear before you, giving rise to a new hope found in each calling to and calling from relationships, places and experiences. With no apology you acknowledge your desire for More and your passion for "This, That or It" surfaces, revealing itself in a very personal and impactful way. Seeing yourself as worthy of More, as you stand today, is often the greatest of life's mountains that only Love can help you climb over or tunnel through. So I have a personal daily prayer that I pray each and every morning that I have adapted from a Christian scripture in Paul's letters to the Ephesians.

> *Creator and Great Love in my life,*
> *Help me to see that I am enough for whatever comes*
> *my way today, enlighten the eyes of my heart so that I*
> *will know the hope found in my callings, bestirring my*
> *own understanding and knowledge that I am the perfect*
> *expression of a divine love, purpose, joy and wisdom.*

We each are challenged with finding a safe place where we can give ourselves permission to be still, listen, reflect and listen some more. Some areas that a soul dive will call you to give your attention to will be uncomfortable and hard to face, and you may want and need extra support. Understand that not everyone has earned the right to hear your story and quite frankly, most will not be ready to. It is important that you have someone that you can talk openly with who is willing to, and knows how to, love and support you through this. Let me repeat! It is very important that you have someone who not only is willing to, but also knows how to love and support you through this journey. If your dive needs to be explored with a professional, gift yourself with this resource. It is critical that you know where you can reach out and find the support you need through any dive. I initially talked to the very few family members and friends with whom I felt safe and they helped some, but there was a growing awareness in me, that this demanded a deeper conversation.

There comes a time when you need to go to a higher power for answers, direction and guidance; you need to look to that which is greater than yourself alone. Whatever your spiritual practice, there is a Divine Love that calls us all into a sacred connectedness. This requires that we be vulnerable and open to a divine dialog. Again, do not hesitate to seek out someone to help guide you in understanding and working through all that surfaces. I cannot stress enough that what worked for me or will work for someone else may be very different from what works for you. So find what helps you best and do not be afraid to step out on faith into the deeper waters of your spirituality, which will most assuredly take you outside of your comfort zone. Hopefully you have already begun using the reflection questions provided and are having compassionate discussions of self-reflection. Take some time and revisit your responses. Capture your own wisdom surfacing by writing a paragraph or two reflecting on your feelings, thoughts and emotions towards what you have read. Remember, this is not an exercise in judging or beating yourself up. It is taking the opportunity to be attentive and present to what is being offered. Listen to the love, forgiveness, encouragement, and hope being spoken to you as you remain open to More.

Breathe, take an even deeper breath, and let's dive.

How can I support myself as I continue to dive into the tender and delicate areas of my life? What can I free myself of to support me in my dives?

(Refer to the workbook, pages 59-60, for an even deeper dive into self-reflection.)

REFLECTION 4: LISTEN TO HEAR

*I will listen to hear, not limiting myself to the pleasure
of self confirmation. I will listen for all the joyful sounds
of a renewed vision, vulnerable to a strengthened faith
that is beyond a belief in mere possibilities.*

Your Soul Dive journey offers a cobblestone pathway toward greater hope and love to which you awaken stone by stone. It is a time of rediscovery that not only requires you to bravely practice a wholehearted love, but will also demand patience and a willingness to listen in ways you may not be so familiar with. As you work to grow in greater understanding and enter into times of self-reflection, you will be challenged to become not only responsive, but also a more attentive listener. Entire books have been written about the art of listening and the awakening that comes with contemplative prayer and discernment, so don't be too hard on yourself if listening does not come easily to you at first.

As I began my own Soul Dive in search of my Happiness, I can remember feeling a bit lost when it came to listening for divine direction and guidance. I know God is real and ever present in my life, but allowing myself to trust and believe that I was worthy of or important enough for divine dialog was a bit overwhelming. Offering my own response was challenging, but I knew I could find the time and space to quiet myself so that I could respond from my heart and not just from the first thoughts that came to mind. But listening for a response from God, my Inner Voice, the Creator, Source, Divine Wisdom or however you choose to identify, this was different. Quite frankly, I could not seem to hear anything, and the harder I tried to listen, the more deafening the silence became.

Understanding the difference between offering my time and taking time to listen was a lesson that helped me greatly along this journey. This is a lesson in surrendering to a discerning ear that hears beyond the practical, reasonable and familiar. Offering our time says we are willing to be present to possibility and movement in a way that may not be familiar or within any schedule we have created. We listen not to hear what to do next, but to be stirred into a discovery of who we are choosing to be. Very often, we try to decide on the perfect time and prepare the perfect place to sit comfortably and be quiet. We put on relaxing music, burn our favorite candles and sit in silence waiting for the magic to happen. This is how this lesson came to me.

I have always cherished the few minutes of bliss I have early in the morning when my eyes first open and I feel all the possibility of having the best day of my life cuddling with me. Something about the warmth of a good slumber just comforts and loves on me something fierce. As

I was going through a time of discernment in my life, I knew I had to find some time to "Listen." I was learning that listening is a critically important part of discernment, and because of my busy schedule I needed to carve out some time to be still, quiet myself, and listen. So I did just that. I took time and began getting right up in the morning to prepare to listen. I would make sure I went to the bathroom because I didn't want to interrupt God with a bathroom break. I would get my coffee, get my neck roll and my favorite throw. I lit a candle and sat, trying to be as attentive as possible. God had my undivided attention and I was ready to hear all God had to say to me. The result: silence, more silence, deafening silence. I was now rushing to get to work on time because the time seemed to fly by. My entire day just seemed rushed and out of whack somehow. I actually did this for a couple of weeks and finally realized that this was not working. It was in this moment and saying those words when I heard that familiar voice in the center of my chest say, "Give me my time back."

It was as if my memory had been put on pause and then someone hit the play button and the music was playing again. I suddenly awakened to the fact that this divine voice of love and goodness has always spoken to me. It was in those few moments lying in the bliss of the waking up; it was in the song that I suddenly could not get out of my head while washing dishes; or in the conversations I have in my car when I am free to sound silly and sing loud and off key. But those were moments I had no hand in creating, just the "yes" that followed the request. So now I lie there just a few extra moments welcoming the best morning conversation ever, opening myself up to hear that gentle voice throughout the entire day. And strangely enough, I am never late and never rushed. It is as if time is standing still for me.

Listening is not only done in the 20 minutes of your choosing, it is an unceasing prayer of being open to all that is to be heard – my fifth Nugget. I do have a favorite place that I like to go that is peaceful and where I can quiet myself quite nicely, but I still most often hear the loving voice of the Creator on my walks to the coffee shop or in the moments before I get out of bed in the morning, and my mind has had a chance to fill up with the things I must get done throughout the day. It is in these moments that I have no hand in planning that I am able to truly offer myself to listen with my whole being. Folks who have control issues will truly struggle with this one. No worries. I feel your pain, but please know offering your time means being available without the "only ifs" and demands we normally make on the things needing our attention. Let me just say that the idea that you are willing to listen between 6 a.m. and 7 a.m. on Tuesdays and Thursdays is not going to fly, and exhausting yourself with all the extra preparation can be unnecessary. Offer time to listen, take time to respond.

Growing in your ability to listen and discern what you are hearing will support your travels more deeply inward, revealing more fully your authentic self. In his book *Falling Upward*, Father Richard Rohr explains that he knows he can say something one way and it will be heard "on as many as ten different levels, depending upon the inner psychological and spiritual maturity of the listener." As a side note, Father Rohr is a Franciscan priest who has no idea that he helped saved me from leaving my faith at the basement steps. That is a novel in itself and while I will leave that story for another day, I will take the opportunity to say "Thank you Father Rohr."

Becoming mindful of the fact that what we hear can be distorted depending on our mental, emotional and spiritual self-awareness is crucial for a discerning listener. We must be responsive to the fact that what we hear initially may not always be received as it was intended. So throughout a deep dive, to assume that the first emotion that stirs up in your belly or the first thought that pops into your head is all there is, as strong as they may be, can leave your "This, That or It" a forever mystery.

You should never apologize for being vigorously attentive to taking the necessary time and energy to cultivate your awareness of and connectedness to "This, That or It" calling out for your attention. There is no pre-set formula or rigid timeframe for any of this, only a guarantee that there will be a demand on you to listen, respond, listen more, expand your response and listen some more. You will have moments when you think to yourself with confidence, "I got it." Then you will continue to listen and work through it, and with a soul full of renewed joy and wisdom, you will come to realize with even greater confidence "I know nothing." Allow your heart to break open, exposing your very soul in authentic love, and listen with an expectation that all of creation is listening with you. This may sound out of reach, but it is truly only a breath away.

I must admit I still have moments or days when the gentle voice is silent. It is here, in this silence, that I must remind myself to let go and be present to the now and open simply to hear what is being offered. Most recently for me, it was when sitting in the darkest of nights on a wooden bench oceanside in the Mexican Riviera listening to the crashing waves filling the night air. I just sat there on my bench, enjoying the ocean sounds, the cool breeze, and seeking nothing, and then it happened. I became profoundly aware that for weeks an old hymn from church had been playing over and over again in my head. Giving in to the urging within my heart I just began to sing:

Come by here my Lord, come by here
Come by here my Lord, come by here
Come by here my Lord, come by here
Oh Lord, come by here

…and then I heard the familiar voice piercing my heart singing back to me……

Come By Here My Child, Come By Here
Come By Here My Child, Come By Here
Come By Here My Child, Come By Here
Oh Precious Child Of Mine, Come By Here

I allowed the tears to fall and my heart to break open and with renewed joy and perfect harmony I sang, "I am here Lord, I am here!"

Breathe in the love being offered and dive in!

Is there a song that you find that you cannot get out of your head? What are the exact words you find yourself singing over and over again? What might these lyrics be speaking to you?

(Refer to the workbook, pages 61-62, for an even deeper dive into self-reflection.)

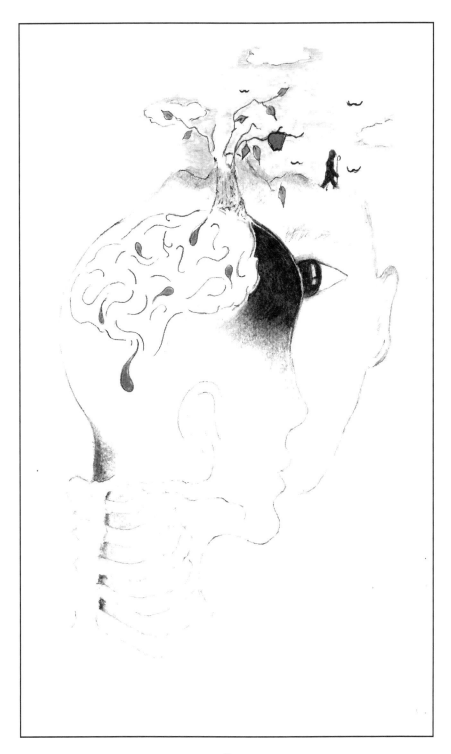

REFLECTION 5: BE STIRRED

To bestir Connectedness one must be willing to be seen,
heard and felt, embracing the uncertainty of
a posture of Authentic Love, acknowledging
that what I do with my life matters.

We are more than sideline participants in this thing called life, and our innermost gifts and beauty can remain hidden when we choose to linger at the perimeter. We are co-creators challenged to be conscious of what we are allowing and disallowing into our lives. It is important to understand that what you do with your life matters and what I do with my life matters and that at some level the ripple effects of our individual choices are felt at our oneness. Even when the story is all about you or all about me, it is never solely about you or me. There is always another story being lived out; a something else happening somewhere else, whether you are aware of it or witness to it.

Our struggle to be faithful to the sacred tapestry into which we are woven at our conception is not to be dismissed; it is real and finding our way to be present is no effortless task. We are connected one to another, and without an awareness of and gratefulness for this most sacred connectedness, our authentic self, our very best self will remain hidden. Becoming conscious of just how much each of us matter, as individuals and collectively, was a wow moment for me. For some of you this will appear overwhelming and a bit much. Many will look at this as a burden and want to deny the responsibilities being in communion can demand. There is significance in understanding that the choice can appear ambiguous, but the response is always a simple yes or no. Again, every ripple is ultimately created by our yeses and our noes to opportunities to love and be loved. A revelation of love and compassion can rebuild and restore those things thought to be lost, and this is a power we must work to grasp. We are all meant to return to the enchantment of our best selves, which will always encourage us to embrace the great love that our sacred and intimate connection to God and to each other gifts us. I love this quote by James Thurber, "*Let us not look back in anger, nor forward in fear, but around in awareness.*"

To bestir Awareness one must be open
to the divine inspiration of ones callings, knowing
there is always more going on, and standing in the courage of
being present in sacred connectedness, refusing to wear the
mask of denial and avoidance.

Our sacred connectedness tasks us to grow in our awareness of the passionate presence of God in all of life, and to find the great love waiting for us to show up in the ordinary events of our lives, work and play. The very nature of our spirituality acknowledges the power and presence of a greater understanding than ours alone. Divine wisdom is always beckoning each of us toward our "This, That or It," challenging us to stand in grateful awareness of ourselves, present to the More happening all around us. A greater sense of awareness gives rise to an empowering accountability and encourages us into a loving relationship with Wisdom, Purpose and Joy. If you could look back and remember the moment you awakened to a desire for More, I would bet there was some self-accountability alert happening somewhere in your life.

I love the ancient Cherokee legend of the two wolves. It presents a picture of a grandfather teaching his grandson a life lesson about the internal fight between good and evil. According to the legend, the grandfather tells his grandson, "A fight is going on inside me. It is a terrible fight and it is between two wolves. One is evil – he is anger, envy, sorrow, regret, greed, arrogance, self-pity, guilt, resentment, inferiority, lies, false pride, superiority, self-doubt, and ego. The other is good – he is joy, peace, love, hope, serenity, humility, kindness, benevolence, empathy, generosity, truth, compassion, and faith. This same fight is going on inside you – and inside every other person, too." The grandson thought about it for a minute and then asked his grandfather, "Which wolf will win?" The old chief simply replied, "The one you feed."

What a powerful testimony to accountability and understanding that what we do matters. Awareness opens up the doors to rediscovery and, as the soul begins to stir, your More surfaces in gratitude, demanding your attention.

To bestir gratefulness, one must let go of the attitude of entitlement and the unwillingness to forgive; to be grateful not only for one's gifts and talents but also for one's deficiencies and imperfections, knowing that they invite us to the faithful mystery of sacred connectedness.

We bestir gratefulness as a way of being when we see beyond the individual roles of giver and receiver, and in thanksgiving, recognize the fellowship of the two. Recognizing the interdependency of the giver and receiver urges you to see gratitude not only in your appreciation for what you have obtained, but even more in what you have been allowed to sow into. Sowing always has an expectation of more. We sow a seed hoping it will grow to its highest potential so that we can taste and enjoy the gifts of its fruit. Whether it is a rose bush offering beauty to the landscape, fresh tomatoes offering us nutrition or our children offering us love, each seed planted has gifts we hope to receive.

In all things sown, we recognize that the fruits we seek come at the cost of an intentional destroying of the seed planted, and even in this struggle we find joy and thanksgiving. Gratefulness is not limited to an appreciation for our personal haves and have nots, it encourages the full embrace of loving all that we are and are not. Gratefulness sees our imperfections as the soul links to God and to each other, and invites each of us into the faithful mystery of God with Us. This journey provides opportunity upon opportunity for our gaps to be filled and our brokenness to be healed. Our life space in Something

More gratefully acknowledges the gifts of divine wisdom, joy, purpose and love sown into each of us through our oneness. We realize that striving for individual perfection is striving for defeat, and that our "This, That or It" is found as we embrace the priceless understanding that we are worthy of the effort and fight. Accepting the risk and call to love, who we are, pressures our More to surface. I believe it is this pressure that shapes and helps to define our deepest passion and desire. As I said earlier, knowing our darkness defines our light, and knowing pain and hurt gives our laughter significance and builds our appreciation for peace.

The divine and omnipotent love that mysteriously binds us one to another and calls us into fellowship will meet you where you are. However, you choose to identify that which is greater than yourself, know this great loving wisdom can never be compromised or diminished to accommodate your lack. Lack of understanding, lack of patience, lack of faith, lack of willingness; whatever the lack, it is just that, your lack not God's. As sad as this may be, we rarely embrace this love fully, until we have a tragedy before us or some deep-rooted pain we cannot ease on our own.

I want you to imagine yourself walking through an amusement park and suddenly you see the largest water ride in the park. You are watching all the people on and around the ride and observing the effects of the water splashing on them. At this position you are a "spectator." Although you are just a spectator, you may find yourself laughing at the people and getting some pleasure from simply observing the experience. Now I want you to imagine yourself moving in closer to that same water ride. Suddenly you feel the mist. Standing in this mist, it feels wonderful and cools you off, under the blaring sun without you getting completely wet. In this position you are affected but undisturbed and you may have no urge to move closer. Now, imagine moving in even closer to this same water ride. The mist has turned into droplets of water splashing you and wetting your hair and clothes. Although the cool water feels great, you recognize the effects are greater and you begin to negotiate, asking yourself, "Do I return to the mist or do I continue to allow the water to fall on me?" Here you must decide if the change from dry hair to wet hair, dry clothes to wet clothes, dry shoes to squishy shoes is what you want. In this position you are no longer a spectator only and you are called to be more aware.

Now, imagine yourself on the ride. As your boat comes down the steep hill you are drenched from the various waterfalls you encounter. The effects of the water are even greater, and you are completely soaked. It will be hours before you are dry again even if the sun stays out and well, let's just say it is time to visit the gift shop and buy a hat. Are you beginning to see? The water has never changed from being H_2O but its effects on you personally are determined by where you have positioned yourself and what you are willing to experience; willing to be present to. Whether a misty breeze or an all-out drenching, water is still two parts hydrogen and one part oxygen. How it affects you, what it becomes in your experience is determined only by where you choose stand.

I must tell you that when I decide to take those steps towards More, it stirred me and gave me a shake in the most unexpected ways. This ride is going to mess up your hair and get your face real twisted, so be ready my friend, be ready. It is a great task but your willingness to be fully present to your current position and posture are key. The journey towards More calls you to an authentic acknowledgment of what you are asking, looking and yearning for, so that you can be accountable to where this ride is taking you.

To bestir authenticity, you must be willing
to fearlessly fall in love with and be loved by
yourself – letting go of who you think you should be,
what the world has molded you to impersonate,
and become fully present to who you are.

So, is the "This, That or It" journey leading you towards something to be obtained or attained? Is your Something More as simple as an awakening to a deeper love of self? Could the letting go of who you think you should be and what the world has molded you to impersonate be what allows you to become fully present to who you truly are? Are the falling masks the key to accepting the gifts of your "This, That or It"? Yes, yes, yes and yes. Taking the courageous steps to open your soul and fearlessly fall in love with and value all that you are and are not, will reveal all that you are in search of.

We seek that which we already are. We are beckoned back to authentic purpose, joy and wisdom, all rooted in a deep seeded need to love and be loved. Who I am and who you are, behind the labels life puts on us is where the soul resides and where we can fully embrace and enjoy More. We must risk the fall, and free ourselves from the love limits of unforgiveness, self-doubt, shame, fear and guilt. Doing so allows us the wisdom that gives significance and resolve to our struggles and our challenges. We gratefully look toward this sacred longing calling us to be alert to our "This, That or It," and we dare to love in spite of what the hurt, perceived failures and betrayals tell us we should avoid.

With vociferous harmony, allow the sacred song of your heart to be heard, and dim your light for no one. Listen attentively for the soul melody that threads each of us into sacred connectedness. It gently and quietly plays the notes as our creator offers them, keeping us in fellowship with each other and with God. It is here in this purest expression of love that we realize our deepest desires, sweetest dreams and humbling wisdom. It is here that we find our most authentic selves, clothed in purposeful destiny.

My hope and prayer is that throughout these pages you have been encouraged to go after your "This, That or It," your Something More. That you take a soul dive or two, or three or ten, and listen, respond and listen some more. That you discover your precious life-giving Nuggets and dare to Love the God who is with you and in you. Let the great bestirring of yourself towards a connectedness to, awareness of, and gratefulness for your most authentic self, your best self, present to the source of all divine wisdom, begin. As you begin to stir and you feel like you are missing out on something big or that you are failing to keep some long-standing appointment, allow yourself to go deeper into the More space of your life, and with no apology and a refreshed wisdom, joyfully shout, YES! I wholeheartedly believe that this journey is an ascending one that will raise you up to your highest potential, where you will find a passionate courage to face your very soul, and with a gentle kiss say I LOVE YOU AND I TRUST YOU!

Take a deep breath and take a minute to just be with the words I love you and I trust you!

Given where you stand today, what are you connected to? What are you aware of? What are you grateful for?

(Refer to the workbook, pages 63-66, for an even deeper dive into self-reflection.)

THE SOUL DIVE WORKBOOK
Includes Soul Dive Bank of Questions

Reflection 1: Something More

1. Reflect on the following quote:

"There is an unceasing longing to connect to, grow in awareness of, and be grateful for the inherent divine reality that our cultivated reality tends to contradict."

2. What am I yearning for? How would I identify the "This, That or It" I am seeking?

3. What are my Nuggets of Truth? How/Where do I allow these Nuggets to support me in my everyday life?

Nugget #1 _____

This truth supports me when _____

_____

Nugget #2 _____

This truth supports me when _____

_____

Nugget #3 _____

This truth supports me when _____

_____

Nugget #4 _____

This truth supports me when _____

_____

Nugget #5 _____

This truth supports me when _____

_____

4. What are some of the untruths that continue to show up in my life? How can my Nuggets speak back to these untruths?

5. What do I dream about? What am I passionate about? How and where do my dreams and my passions show up in my life?

Reflection 2: Dare To Love

1. Reflect on the following quote:

    "My purpose, wisdom and joy will be revealed the moment I bravely look towards love and dare to say 'Hello.'"

2. When, where and with whom do my feelings of being unloved emerge?

3. What are my Love Limits? How do I respond to the emotions, hurts, and disappointment of feeling unloved?

4. How do these limits hinder my ability to fully embrace my "This, That or It – Something More?"

5. In the heart below write out those things you hold sacred and allow to take up residency in your heart (people, things, places, etc.). Then include your love limits from Question 3 in the space framing your heart and limiting your ability to love fully.

Reflection 3: Deep Dive

1. Reflect on the following quote:

   "The road traveled in joyful purpose will most certainly gift you with a selfie. Who I am and where I stand today is an unavoidable reality I shall find the courage to embrace."

2. If someone were to write a book about me today, what would the title be? _____

   _____

Explain:

3. When is the last time I felt a true sense of awe? Where was I? How old was I?

4. What am I witness to? What do I see, hear and experience? How and where does what I witness show up in my life?

5. Where are the empty places in my heart? How and where does this emptiness show up in my life?

Reflection 4: Listen To Hear

1. Reflect on the following quote:

    "I will listen to hear, not limiting myself to the pleasure of self con-firmation. I will listen for all the joyful sounds of a renewed vision, being vulnerable to a strengthened faith that is beyond a belief in mere possibilities."

2. How do I hear the voice of divine wisdom? I can I be more open to hear this voice?

    Is this a voice I trust? Why do I trust or distrust this voice?

3. What song do I find myself singing for no reason at all? What does this song say to me?

4. In what areas of my life could I listen more attentively? What message could I be missing in these situations?

Reflection 5: Be Stirred

1. Reflect on the following quote:

   "To bestir Connectedness one must be willing to be seen, heard and felt, embracing the uncertainty of a posture of Authentic Love, acknowledging that what I do with my life matters."

2. Where am I seen, heard and felt? To whom am I fully present? What does this look like in my life?

3. Reflect on the following quote:

   "To bestir gratefulness one must let go of the attitude of entitlement and the unwillingness to forgive; to be grateful not only for one's gifts and talents but also for one's deficiencies and imperfections, knowing that they invite us to the faithful mystery of sacred connectedness."

4. Where do I see judgement as a factor in my inability to receive the gift of my More?

On a separate piece of paper write down the people, places, things or experiences you are most grateful for. Include a thank you prayer, note, or poem in your own words. Physically, mentally and spiritually carry this note of gratitude with you over the next week.

5. What makes me laugh uncontrollably?

6. What makes me cry? What makes my heart ache?

7. Where am I my most creative? Am I allowing space for my creativity to be expressed?

8. Reflect on the following quote:

   "To bestir authenticity you must be willing to fearlessly fall in love with and be loved by yourself – letting go of who you think you should be (what the world has molded you to impersonate) and become fully present to who you are."

9. When am I my most authentic self? In what ways do I honor him/her? In what ways do I dismiss him/her?

MY AWESOME VILLAGE

I am so blessed to be supported, loved and poured into by a village of family and friends. Some I have chosen and some have chosen me.

To my parents, Tom and Trayia, who have loved and encouraged me to be the seeker I am. Daddy, even though you and Grandma have passed, I know you are both watching over me, helping and supporting me every step of the way. Mom you are truly awesome and I love you!

To my gifted brother Tommy, you are one of the most God loving men I know. Please never allow anyone to steal the Joy, Love and Wisdom that God offers to YOU. You are so special to me and I am honored to call you my brother.

To my wonderful Aunts Bunny and Jacquie who have been my greatest teachers of courageous love, forgiveness and joyful mischief; to my aunts, Deborah and Jo, cousins Johnny, Marianne, Sheila, Mary Alice and my sisters from another mother, Liza, Tracy and Valerie and my brother Mr. James Lewis. I love my mini me, Payton, nieces

Macy and Brooklynn so much; to the phenomenal women of my Circle of Sisters, Bakhita Dance Ministry, Women's Bible Study and parish family of Saint Dominic Catholic Church and the Dominican Sisters of Peace, I say thank you, thank you, thank you. I love you all to pieces! Each of you have supported me and taught me how to dare to love and be loved.

To Kimberly and Charlene, I cannot express my appreciation enough for all you have invested in me. You leant me your talents, skills and creativity and I am so blessed to have you both in my live.

To the spiritual sisters, mothers and friends in my life, Fran Frazier, Sister Pat Dual OP, Sister Carol Ann Spencer OP, and Grace Neely. You have cried with me, laughed with me and taught me so much. You have guided me and allowed me to grow and become the loving mess you see today. You have helped me to live from a joyful posture of praise and loved me through it all. Now how do I thank someone for that?

I pray that I can someday be for someone else what you each have been for me. Thank you.

Bibliography, Citations and Notes:

Brown, Brené, Ph.D., L.M.S.W., *The Gift of Imperfection: let go of who you think you're supposed to be and embrace who you are.* (Minnesota: Hazeldon 2010).
> This book in collaboration with Brené Brown's eCourse in Oprah Winfrey's O eCourse series is where I gained my understanding and usage of "Permission Slips."

Rohr, Richard, *Falling Upward: a spirituality for the two halves of life.* (California: Jossey-Bass An Imprint of Wiley 2011).

Come By Here, *Lead Me, Guide Me*, Second Edition (Chicago, GIA Publications, Inc. 2000)
> Tune: DESMOND, 8885; Negro Spiritual arranged by Evelyn Simpson- Curenton, b. 1953 copyright 2000, GIA Publications, Inc.

Two Wolves – Cherokee Parable
Parable found on the *Pearls Of Wisdom: Awakening Personal and global Consciousness* website at:
www.sapphyr.net/natam/two-wolves.htm
Author Unknown (possibly a Cherokee parable, and going back probably at least to the 1950's in print - but un-confirmable.)

All Biblical and Scriptural references and texts were taken from: The Catholic Bible, Personal Study Edition NAB (New York, Oxford University Press 1995).

All featured artwork was created specifically for this project and was donated by the artist, Thomas E. Pannell Jr.

Cover photo was taken by Andrea Pannell at the Present Moment Retreat in Troconos Beach, Mexico.

ABOUT THE AUTHOR

ANDREA PANNELL is on a mission to encourage us all to become passionately engaged in life, challenging us to reach for the Something More starving for our attention. Andrea feels connecting with our deepest stirrings is never disappointing and will ultimately become our guide into our desired life. A dynamic speaker and retreat leader, Andrea is a creative soul who values all forms of artistic expression and believes creativity is one of the great testimonies to the presence of God. An active parishioner of St. Dominic Catholic Church, Andrea is a member of the Bakhita Dance Ministry and the Gospel Choir, and sees her faith community as essential to her spiritual health. Andrea leads a Circle of Sisters that has been meeting for over three years, that continues to provide a safe and supportive environment for women looking to rediscover their best selves. She is also a REAL Women of the Rise Sister Rise Network that provides opportunities to support and work towards placing Black girls at promise. Andrea has lived in three countries and loves traveling to the less touristy parts of the world. Currently she works in the field of development in the city where she was born and raised, Columbus, Ohio. She has one adult son and looks forward to discovering the adventures God offers with each new day. Visit Andrea at her website, www.ThePannellGroup.com for more information and bookings.